Brian Moses presents his poetry and percussion show in schools, libraries and theatres. He lives in a small Sussex village where he regularly walks his dog, who is often surprised to see him jumping streams, climbing hills and running along river banks in the mistaken belief that should the Olympic committee invite him to take part in the games he will be fit enough to go for gold! Contact Brian via his website: www.brianmoses.co.uk

When **Roger Stevens** was younger, he played football and tennis, but now he watches sport on television. Roger thinks that philately should be included in the Olympics, as he once did win a gold medal for his stamp collection.

He is the author of many children's books, including four solo collections of poems for Macmillan Children's Books, anthologies, novels and much more besides.

When not writing, Roger performs in a band and visits schools, festivals and libraries performing his poems, making people laugh and encouraging everyone to read more poetry. Visit his award-winning website at www.poetryzone.co.uk

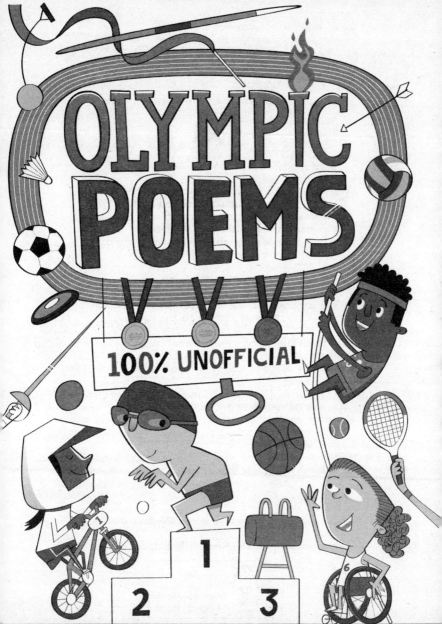

OLYMPIC POEMS

100% UNOFFICIAL

★ Brian Moses and Roger Stevens ★

Illustrated by Nathan Reed

MACMILLAN CHILDREN'S BOOKS

The Olympic Games

'The most important thing is not to win
but to take part'

Bishop of Pennsylvania, 1908

First published 2012 by Macmillan Children's Books

This edition published 2021 by Macmillan Children's Books
an imprint of Pan Macmillan
EU representative: Macmillan Publishers Ireland Limited,
Mallard Lodge, Lansdowne Village, Dublin 4
Associated companies throughout the world
www.panmacmillan.com

ISBN 978-1-5290-4301-3

1 3 5 7 9 8 6 4 2

A CIP catalogue record for this book is available from the British Library.

Printed and bound by CPI Group (UK) Ltd, Croydon CR0 4YY

Contents

For our 2016 Olympic athletes (BM)

For Lily, Ruby, Merlin and Sam (RS)

This poem is nervous to begin with.
All the other poems look fit, confident,
sure they can do it,
sure they can flit through these pages
at lightning speed.
But the sound of a gun signals the off
and words run
> *hither*
and
> *thither*
for a moment until they collect themselves
and fall into a rhythm . . .

Moving fast
Make no mistake
This marathon's
A piece of cake
I'm proper chipper
Nippy, zippy
I've seams and reams
Of energy
For my next trick
I'm electric
Like a striker
On a hat-trick
Ducking, diving
Through the pages
How I love
These early stages.   *. . . to be continued*

1

Advice for Staging Your Own Olympic Games

Never play volleyball with a bag of flour
Never use Mum's hairbrush as a baton in the
  relay race
The flower-bed is not a sandpit for the long
  jump
And remember – the Olympic Games does not
  include kiss-chase

Never pole-vault in the vicinity of Grandpa's
  greenhouse
Never throw the discus using Mum's best
  plates
The broom handle is not a pole – nor is it a
  javelin
Never use flowerpots (especially if they have
  flowers in) for weights

Your dog is a dog, not a horse
Although, at a push, could be used for
  equestrian events
Do not use the duvet covers in the airing
  cupboard
To make those big marquee-type tents

Never use the complete set of Delia Smith for
the winners' podium
Never bribe the judges with crisps, chocolate,
football cards or cash.
And finally when Mum comes home to find
her house and garden in a mess
Say, Excuse me, but I'm in the hundred
metres – must dash!

Roger Stevens

To Be an Olympic Athlete . . .

You need a lion's heart
and a swift pair of feet,
to be a champion
Olympic athlete.

You need exercise,
so get off the settee,
jog in the park
instead of watching TV.

You need a fire in your eyes
that never goes out,
no room at all
for any moment of doubt.

You need a real hunger
to go out and win,
you need a resolve
to never give in.

You need to break through
that barrier of pain,
and a mantra that tells you to
'train, train, train'.

Then one day, who knows,
to the sound of applause,
you will stand on the steps
and the gold will be yours.

Brian Moses

Athlete

Fast runner
Never give upper
Hard trainer
Careful eater
Stop watcher
Dawn catcher
Muscle stretcher
Dream follower
Team member
Record maker
Gold winner

Roger Stevens

Sporting Definitions

Dressage – how long it takes to get ready

Fencing – building a wooden barrier around the stadium

Greece – the name of the film where John Travolta invented Olympic dancing

High Jumper – badly knitted garment by Granny

Long Jumper – (see High Jumper)

Triple Jump – a visit by three ghosts

Parallel Bars – two pubs exactly opposite one another on a street

Pole Vault – jumping over someone from Poland

Rowing – argument

Shuttlecock – male chicken going backwards and forwards between two hens

Water Polo – small mint dropped in pool

Roger Stevens

The Overtaker

I'm an overtaker,
off down the line.
I don't wait around.
I haven't got time.

I'm an overtaker,
I can't stay back.
I'm out in front
ahead of the pack.

Better keep clear
in the swimming bath.
Everybody
out of my path.

I'm an overtaker,
watch me run.
Every sports day,
sound of the gun.

There I go,
off down the track.
Nothing is going
to hold me back.

Head in the clouds,
I don't look round,
keep my feet
clear of the ground.

Run to school
every day,
any old race,
I'm OK.

Dash home at night,
have lots of fun.
I'm an overtaker,
watch me r . . . . un!

Brian Moses

Winning

I once thought it was all about winning,
but it's not.

I once thought I could win easily,
and I could,

till the day I raced with David Fleming.
David who was teased and tormented.
David who had nothing going for him.

David, just behind me,
straining and aching to win . . .

And I could have won so easily,
I could have . . .

But I didn't.

I pretended to be hurt,
slipped, clutched my ankle,
let him win.

Watched the grin spread
over his face.

I let David Fleming
win the race

and it felt
so good.

Brian Moses

11

Slow Motion

In television
High-definition
Slow motion
The facial muscles pull
Seem to disfigure the jaw
And a bead of sweat
Like a free-falling diamond
In the weightlessness of space
Catches the sun

Roger Stevens

Sprint

The air is hot. The sky is blue. Expect
No favours from the sun. You stand alone.
Survey the stadium, the crowd. Inspect
The track. A moment's doubt. Can it be done?

And then the training – days, months,
    years – kicks in
And you are focused on the prize. You know
With certainty what you must do. Begin
With deep breaths. Stretch. Relax. It's time
    to go.

A billion eyes are watching. You can't hide.
There's silence. You can hear your beating
    heart.
You crouch. Into the starting blocks you slide.
You wait. Time stops. You hope there's no
    false start.

Marks. Get set. Kick. Ten seconds and you're
    done.
You are the bullet in the starter's gun.

Roger Stevens

Running the Marathon

I'm going to run the marathon,
wearing a diving suit,
strapped to a parachute.
With a cloak and staff like Noah,
pushing a garden mower.
In a ballet dancer's tutu,
cracking a cowboy's lasso.
Yes, I'm going to run the marathon,
inside a suit of armour,
leading a Tibetan llama.
As an ancient prince from Khartoum,
in a Loch Ness Monster costume.
As Adam running from Eve,
or a camel from Tel Aviv.
Yes, I'm going to run the marathon,
As a green and grotty ogre,
in an Imperial Roman toga.
As a bridegroom on his wedding day,
or someone dressed to play croquet.
In a dragon costume from China,
as a luxury ocean liner.

Yes, I'm going to run the marathon
and I want to get myself seen.
Although maybe, just maybe,
I think it might be best
to forget all these wacky ideas
and stick with shorts and vest!

Brian Moses

I Am the Fastest

I once ran the hundred metres so fast
All the cheetahs in the local zoo were jealous

I once ran the hundred metres so fast
The friction, as my feet hit the running track,
    set my running shoes on fire

I once ran the hundred metres so fast
I broke the sound barrier

I once ran the hundred metres so fast
I reached the finishing line in the blink of an
    eye
In the click of a finger and thumb
In the time it takes to say Jack Robinson

I once ran the hundred metres so fast
I reached the winning tape before I'd even
    started running

Roger Stevens

A Sub-two-hour Marathon?

A million pounds
for sub two hours
to a marathon runner
with special powers.

It could be the prize
that's big enough.
Sport's holy grail
for someone tough.

It once seemed as unlikely
as reaching the moon,
but experts predict
it could happen soon.

Berlin is the place,
some runners say,
almost at sea level
most of the way.

Good weather will help,
no wind in your face.
With a flat course there's hope
of a record-breaking race.

One fifty-nine, fifty-nine
would do,
and that marathon runner could one day
be YOU!

Brian Moses

Roger Bannister
6 May 1954

It's impossible!
Run a mile in four minutes?
Can't be done, they said

Iffley Road Track in Oxford
Too windy for the record attempt
But the wind suddenly drops

And Roger Bannister
Steps up to the mark
Tall, thin, hair swept back, determined

Three thousand spectators
Raincoats, flat-caps
Will today be the day?

Chris Brasher and Chris Chataway will set
   the pace
Commentary from BBC Radio
Starting pistol and Brasher takes the lead

Bannister is feeling good
His legs full of running
He feels propelled by an unknown force

But they seem to be running too slowly
Bannister shouts, 'Faster!'
But Brasher ignores him and keeps the pace

Half a mile, one minute fifty-eight
Bannister is in his own world, relaxed
Chataway takes over lead

Time to up the pace
And he and Bannister pull away
Three-quarters done, feeling good

The crowd is cheering
The four-minute mile is possible
Can it be done?

On the back straight Bannister takes over
His mind racing ahead, pulling him forward
The final push

He leaps at the tape, he's there
The moment of a lifetime
He feels the record is his

But everyone waits anxiously
Ladies and gentlemen, here is the result
Of event nine, the one mile

A new English Native, British National,
All-comers, European, British Empire
And World Record

The time was three
The roar and joy of the crowd drowns out the
    announcement
Minutes and fifty-nine point four seconds

                              Roger Stevens

Hercules' Gym

Eros, the god of love,
and Ares, the god of war,
are often to be seen
in combat on the floor,

wrestling, one with the other,
each one hoping to win,
but war will never surrender
and love will never give in,

down at Hercules' gym,
we're training
down at Hercules' gym.

And Atlas, statue still,
will advise you on lifting weights,
instructing you how to spin
a pile of tectonic plates.

And then he'll test your strength,
watching you juggle with boulders
till finally you're ready to take
the weight of the world on your shoulders,

down at Hercules' gym,
we're training
down at Hercules' gym.

And you'll meet your fitness trainer,
a shifty guy called Hades,
who thinks he's Mr Universe
and flatters all the ladies.

But if you make Hades mad,
you'll wonder what's got into him
as a swift punch breaks your jaw
and all your lights go dim,

down at Hercules' gym,
we're training
down at Hercules' gym.

And it's best to pretend
you haven't seen
Medusa on
the rowing machine.

Just turn right round
and leave for home
unless you fancy
being turned to stone

down at Hercules' gym,
everybody's going,
down to Hercules' gym.

So visit today, get real,
get a special promotional deal,

down at Hercules' gym,
down at Hercules' gym,
down at Hercules' gym.

(Just tell 'em
Zeus sent you.)

Brian Moses

The Real Battle

On the school field
Or in the Olympic stadium
Your competitors smile
While plotting to beat you
But the real battle
Is in your head

Roger Stevens

Hurdles (1)

Go go go go go go go go jump
Go go go go jump
Go go go go jump
Go go go go jump
Go go go go jump
Go go go go jump
Go go go go jump
Go go go go jump
Go go go go jump
Go go go go jump
Go go go go gogogogo

WIN!

Roger Stevens

Hurdles (2)

Go go go go go go go go jump
Go go go go jump
Go go go go jump
Go go go go jump
Go go go go jump
Go go go go jump
Go go go go jump
Go go go go jump
Go go go go jump
Go go go go trip

Lose

Roger Stevens

The Food Obstacle Race

For school sports day this year
how about trying something different?

Try skipping with spaghetti
    or leaping through lasagne,
diving into doughnuts
    or cartwheeling in ketchup.

Try jumping into jelly
    or battling through bolognese,
somersaulting into sultanas
    or zooming through zabaglione.

Try rowing through rice pudding
    or making waves in mayonnaise,
weightlifting watermelons
    or tiptoeing through tagliatelle.

Try pole-vaulting with pepperoni
    or bouncing on boiled eggs,
stepping in salsa sauce
    or sprinting through salad cream.

And then you should see if your teachers
are up for this challenge too.
The teachers' race will be much more fun
if they do this event just like you!

Brian Moses

Throwing Things

Throwing the hammer
Throwing the discus
Throwing the javelin
There's a lot of throwing in Olympic events

Throwing the race
Throwing a tantrum
Throwing your hat in the air
Throwing a spanner
Throwing a wobbler
Throwing a curved ball
Throwing a chair
Throwing confetti
Throwing spaghetti
Throwing a football
Throwing the match
There's a lot of throwing in Olympic events

And there's usually a catch.

Roger Stevens

Mark Spitz

Everyone remembers
the name Mark Spitz.
True American hero,
they loved him to bitz.

He broke world records
in a bit of a blitz.
Won seven gold medals
then called it quitz.

More than anyone else,
American or Britz.
Bit of an icon
was swimmer Mark Spitz.

Brian Moses

Synchronization

Synchronized swimmers
Shoals of fish in slow motion
Caught in a shaft of light

Roger Stevens

I Never Learned to Dive Like Dave

(For my cousin Dave, five years older than me
and a hero of my childhood)

I never learned to dive like Dave,
I never learned the skill.
In fact I never learned to swim
and now I never will.

But Dave had a way with water
and Dave had a way with waves,
he understood the ebb and flow
of how the sea behaves.

And Dave showed all of Ramsgate
how diving should be done,
competitions entered,
medals and trophies won.

There on the high diving board
you'd see him strain for height,
then calmly jump, flip, rotate
and take his downward flight.

With scarcely a ripple showing
the water would welcome him in.
Dave was a hero to all of us,
an incentive to go out and win.

But I never learned to dive like Dave,
never for me the 'oohs' and 'aahs'
as Dave stood balancing on the board,
arms reaching out to the stars.

Brian Moses

Dive

The thin board beneath your bare feet
Twist twist tuck roll stretch
The unforgiving pool

Roger Stevens

Fish Out of Water

Once a year
Dad has the bright idea
Of a family trip
To the swimming pool
Where he becomes a shark
Gliding below the water's surface
Ready to grab you unawares
And pull you under
In a mass of shrieks and bubbles

Mum is an eel
So beautiful in the water
Twisting and turning
Gliding elegantly
As though born to swim

My sister is a ray
She can hold her breath
For three minutes
And float along the bottom
Of the pool

But what am I?
There is no fish
That makes such a bad job of swimming
That can hardly cross from one side of a pool
To the other
That hates the water
The coldness, the wetness of it
Maybe I am the first fish
Who crawled out of the sea
To breathe air
And live on land

Roger Stevens

Trampolining

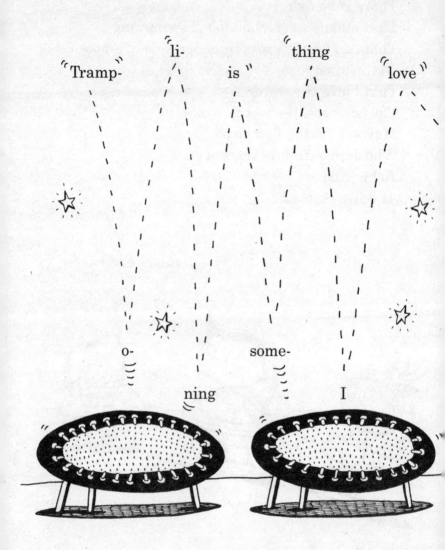

"Tramp- li- is" thing love "

o- some- I

ning

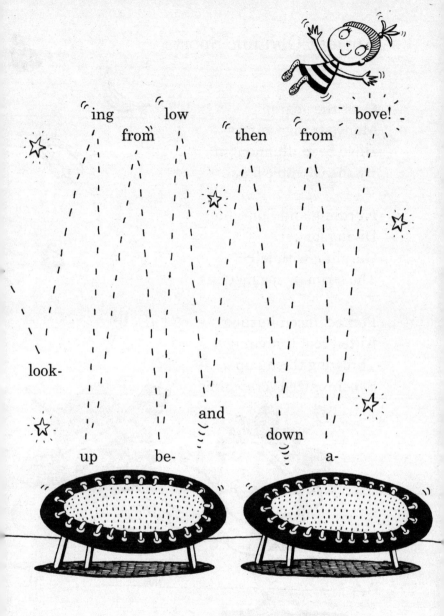

"ing   "low
    from   "then   "from   "bove!

look-

and

down

up   be-   a-

Brian Moses

Ancient Olympic Sports

Over the years
Many strange games
Have been illuminated
By the Olympic flame

Nurdling and Spurgling
Diving for yeti
Gargling with jelly*
The swim in spaghetti

Pantechnicon hurling
Kilted roof-thatching
Throwing the hamper
Synchronized scratching

Vole-vaulting, road-salting
Under-breath mumbling
Hockey on custard
Long-distance grumbling

Most sausages eaten
While running a mile
Oh, how those old sports
Must have once raised a smile

Roger Stevens

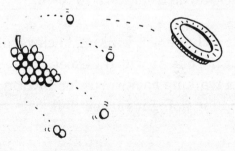

* Poet Brian Patten once won a gold medal in this event!

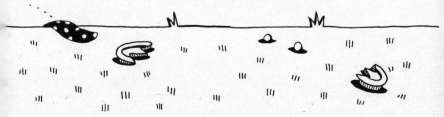

Walking Backwards for Britain

I'm walking backwards for Britain,
Land's End to John o'Groats,
backwards down country lanes
watched only by sheep and goats.

Don't ask me where I'm going,
I concentrate on where I've been,
staring at paths I've followed,
seeing places I've already seen.

Bit of a task walking backwards
making sure that I don't fall down.
Lots of skill required when travelling
backwards from town to town.

It's a challenge, walking backwards,
but it's one at which I excel.
I'm walking backwards for Britain
and I'm doing it rather well.

Brian Moses

Snail Race

To organize a snail race

Draw a starting line
On the path
In chalk

Place a lettuce leaf
One pace away

Show two snails the lettuce
And place snails on the line

Say,
'On your marks, get set,
Go!'

Prepare to be bored.

Roger Stevens

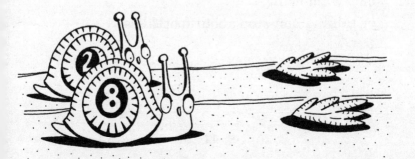

The Lazylympics

Dad's been watching the Olympics.
For the last two weeks we've seen him
take root on our settee,
watching our athletes
do amazing feats
on our TV.

'I'd like to be a medal winner,' he says.
So we thought maybe there could be
an Olympics for lazy people
like Dad.

There could be events like
floating on a lilo in the swimming pool
for the longest time,
or the most ring pulls ripped from
cans of beer.

There could be sports like
thinking about dog-walking,
or lawnmowing,
or talking non-stop about football.

Dad would easily win a medal for yawning,
or eyebrow raising,
or taking a nap that lasts for hours.
And we could be cheerleaders,
cheering Dad on
as he slept his way to victory.

So many things our Dad's good at,
it's just a shame they'll never have
a lazylympics
for sportsmen like Dad.

Brian Moses

Hit a rhythm
Hit a beat
Every syllable complete
Sun or rain
In any weather
Feel like I could rhyme forever

Embryonic, polyphonic
Readers gasp
He's supersonic!
Watch that poem
Helter-skelter
See you later
Ancient reptile
You can use me
As a model
This marathon
Will be a doddle.   *. . . to be continued*

Table Tennis

To play
Table tennis
In our house
You need
A plentiful
Supply
Of balls
As Judydog
Loves to
Join in
By retrieving them
In her mouth
And
Crushing them

Roger Stevens

Fencing

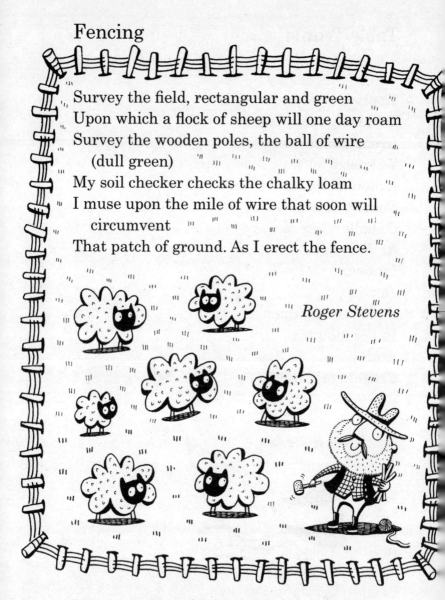

Survey the field, rectangular and green
Upon which a flock of sheep will one day roam
Survey the wooden poles, the ball of wire
    (dull green)
My soil checker checks the chalky loam
I muse upon the mile of wire that soon will
    circumvent
That patch of ground. As I erect the fence.

Roger Stevens

Editor's note: We would like to apologize for this poem.
It seems to have found its way into the wrong book.

The Never-stop-moving Family

The never-stop-moving family
is ruining our holiday,
making us feel really guilty,
we wish that they'd go away.

They're outside before breakfast
doing fifty press-ups each,
then kitted out they're jogging off
for tennis on the beach.

Then it's back for another workout
before jumping on their bikes
or strapping on their rucksacks
and starting ten-mile hikes.

Then it's down to the beach again
with their wetsuits and their boards
and a final session at the gym
just leaves us lost for words.

They must have wings on their ankles
or flames that lick their feet.
Something keeps them powered up,
maybe it's something they eat!

We suspect they've labelled us
the lazy family,
no energy or enthusiasm
for sporting activity.

But we're not here to race about,
face challenges or march up a hill,
we're here for one reason only,
we're simply here to chill!

Brian Moses

Beach Volleyball

(The Queen's response to the news that at the London Olympics 2012 beach volleyball was to be held in Horse Guards Parade, close to the Mall and Buckingham Palace)

Queen Victoria would not have been amused,
she'd never have allowed her parade to be
    used
for activity of such a frivolous sort.
California should be the place for such sport.

The Duke, I know, will not be impressed
with a sport that lacks any class or finesse.
He won't see why those big hunks from the
    States
should be leaping about close to his front
    gates.

It's not the sort of thing that one wants to see.
Why in heavens did nobody tell me?
I would have suggested places more suitable,
Hastings or Brighton, Margate or Whitstable.

Anywhere with a beach would have been the
    right place.
Bringing sand into London is a big disgrace.
It will creep into every cranny and nook
and one thinks how scruffy the Parade will
    look.

I'm going to find out who gave them
    permission
to hold this event and break with tradition.
I'll give the Olympic Committee a call.
It's just not what one does at all.

One rides in one's carriage and waves to the
    crowd,
one troops one's colours and feels very proud.
One certainly doesn't play beach volleyball.
It's just not what one does by the Mall,
not at all,

it's just not what one does by the Mall.

Brian Moses

(NB The word 'Mall' in London is actually pronounced like
'pal' and 'gal' but there weren't any suitable rhymes so I used
what's called 'poetic licence' and made it rhyme with 'ball'.
There's no point in being a poet and having poetic licence if
you don't make use of it sometimes!)

Bonkers About Bikes

You have to be bonkers about bikes
to climb on the back of a Kawasaki
and go.

You have to be crackers
about carburettors,
crankshafts and chains,
mad about machinery
and the manic motion
of tyres on tarmac.

You have to be devoted
to dipsticks and disc brakes,
to be nutty about nuts
whether domed, flanged or
castellated.

You need to be able to talk
about torsion and tension,
sequential transmission and
telescopic forks,
to know about crank oil
and cable chokes,
chains and sprockets,
cable throttles.

You have to be serious about speed,
that need to push faster
than anyone else,
that need to take it to the limit
and then some.

You need to believe
that the knowledge you've gained
will keep you safe.
You need that belief,
that trust,
you and the bike,
the bike and you,

the road ahead,
the sky and the sea,
out in front at
the Isle of Man TT.

Brian Moses

Superlatives

You must be the biggest, the boldest, the best
Superlatives are what you need
If you want Olympic gold
If your dream is to succeed

Highest, furthest, fastest, longest
It's what champions are for
Quickest, hardest, toughest, strongest
Tune your mind to more, more, more

Hungriest, meanest, leanest, keenest
But you can win in other ways
Friendliest, fairest, funkiest, kindest
Better ways to spend your days?

Roger Stevens

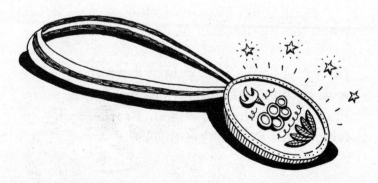

The Greatest

I knew him as Cassius Clay,
you'll know him as Muhammad Ali,
the man who could 'float like a butterfly',
the man who could 'sting like a bee'.

I was never a big fan of boxing
but Ali had plenty to say.
Before every fight he contested
he would offer some witty wordplay.

He'd call his opponent all kinds of names
and tell him how quickly he'd floor him,
while everyone who fought with Ali
just tried their best to ignore him.

And it must have been an amazing day
for wit and repartee,
at a press conference in Miami
when the Beatles met Muhammad Ali.

Ali pretended to knock them down
with both verbal and physical attacks.
Photographs showed all four Beatles
lying at his feet on their backs

'I'm the greatest,' he told them
and he proved it too one night
when he took out Sonny Liston
in the heavyweight title fight.

'It's just a job,' he said.
'Birds fly, waves pound the sand.
I beat people up
with the power of my right hand.'

The man who could 'float like a butterfly',
the man who could 'sting like a bee'.
I knew him as Cassius Clay,
you'll know him as Muhammad Ali.

Brian Moses

Sky Football

Outside a pub
a sign said:
SKY FOOTBALL.

But how do you play
a game like that?

Do you FLY
down the pitch?

Do you boot the ball
into CLOUDS?

Do you dribble it
between STARS?

Do you hear the cheers of ANGELS
as you score a goal?

Just how do you play
SKY FOOTBALL?

Brian Moses

Tennis Match

She looks cool
Bounces ball
Catches my eye
Serves
Thwack
I knock it back
Thwack
Out of reach
Good point
She ups the pace
Thwack
An ace
Umpire's call
Fifteen–all
Thwack
Net
Thwack
Let
Thwack
In
Thwack
Back
Slice, spin
On the line
Thwack
Take that!

She ups the pace
Thwok
Second ace
Umpire's call
Thirty–all
Bounces ball
Thwack
Thwok
Thwack
Scrambles
High lob
Rush cross court
Low volley
Makes shot
I do not
Crowd cheers

Still cool
She bounces ball
Two match points
Thwack
Just out
Moment of doubt
Crowd hushed
High toss
Thwok
Thwack
Thwok
Knock it back

Thwack

Attack
Thwack
Thwack
Thwick
Awkward spin
Quick!
Wild swing
Ball flies
Into sky
Crowd goes crazy
She's on her knees
Jubilation
Hold back tears
Brave smile
Congratulations

Roger Stevens

When poems hit the wall
they fall down,
when poems get puffed
they take a break,
sometimes sit down
at the side of the page
while other lines
with more vigour and verve
swerve round them,
zip past.

Then despite the cheers
from their readers
urging them on
they find it hard
to re-engage,
they need a powerful push
to succeed,
till they're up again
for the final stage,
the last few miles
to smiles and applause
as they head
for home.   *. . . to be continued*

Bicycle Polo

(Bicycle polo made an appearance in the 1908 Olympic Games in London.)

Wouldn't it be great
to have a go
at bicycle
polo?

To twist and turn
your bike about
by trying to give
the ball
a clout.

To swing your mallet
as you try to roll
the ball into
your opponent's
goal.

Then struggle to keep
your bike upright,
your feet off the ground
and the ball
in sight.
Strange to think
that somebody thought
it shouldn't be
an Olympic
sport!

Brian Moses

Looking Up

I wonder why
There are no Olympic airborne sports?
Why are our sights so low?

No flying or ballooning
Microlight or ultralight
Freefall or parachuting

Would the gods
Gazing down from Olympus
Have disapproved?

And will there one day be
Sports in outer space? Or on the moon?
What a high-jump record that would be

Roger Stevens

I'm a Canoe
(*After Flanders and Swann*)

I was thinking about sailing as I strolled along
    a stream
When I met a young man standing by the shore
He was discussing boating trivia with his
    girlfriend called Olivia
And which was best, a paddle or an oar

So I asked, What boat is that? He replied,
    That's a kayak
And I'd have gone on thinking this was true
If the boat of which he spoke hadn't yelled out,
    Please don't joke
A kayak I am not! I'm a canoe

I'm a canoe, I'm a canoe
I'm the c-nicest sort of canoe, how do you do?
I'm a canoe, so don't misconstrue
You really ought to c-know c-who's c-who
I'm not a kayak. I think you should know that
For this chap who thinks I'm that has not a
    c-clue
I don't come from Timbuktu, Kathmandu or
    C-C-Crewe
A fanfare please on your kazoo! I'm a canoe

I'm a canoe, I'm a canoe
And I'm in a slalom race at half past two
I'm a canoe, I'm a canoe
And I'm after an Olympic gold or two
I'm a canoe, a c-nifty canoe
And canoeing is the c-thing that I can do
And so, my friends, to you – adieu, I must away
   to find my crew
I'm not a kayak
C-no, c-no
I am a canoe

Roger Stevens

Archery

Nobody gets excited about archery,
least of all me!
Nobody races the length of the lawns
   screaming
'Gi' us another one.'
Nobody tells the umpire he's blind
when the evidence is there for all to see.
You can't fake a gold ring.

But watching archery is not for me.
It's not a matter for wild celebration,
it's more a matter of contemplation,
concentration, appreciation,
with the margin of victory extremely narrow,
all it takes is one wayward arrow
and the contest is lost.

I just can't get excited about archery,
it's far too quiet a sport for me.
I just don't know what people see
in archery.

Brian Moses

Dead Centre

You stand
Exactly so
Balanced
You grip the bow
Exactly so
To the nearest millimetre
An arrow
Fits snugly
Exactly so
No margin for error
The tension grows
You are unaware
Of the crowds
Of the TV cameras
Of the field
Of the sky
The tension builds
Hold that moment
Like an explosive thought

Let go

The arrow flies
Through twelve thousand years
Of history
To hit the gold
Dead centre

Roger Stevens

White Water

Something tough
that you ought to do
is to race white water
in a swift canoe.

Two metres a second
is the minimum speed,
strength and skill
are what you need

to combat the thrill
of a water burst,
while daring the flood
to do its worst,

till you work with the water
and use its flow
to reach the places
you need to go.

If the gods are with you
you'll make it through
when you race white water
in a swift canoe.

Brian Moses

Super Feats for Super Athletes

As our athletes get fitter and fitter
and so many records keep tumbling
there soon will surely need to be
super feats for super athletes.

Forget the marathon,
the longest run will soon be
along the length of
the Great Wall of China
(a mere 5,500 miles!).

Similar tests of strength and endurance
could include abseiling down the CNN Tower,
swimming the Pacific
with an overnight stop in Hawaii,
surfing tsunami
or bungee jumping from
space stations.

With many people living longer
it may well be possible to see
eighty-year-olds keeping up with
the front runners
or powering their way to
record-breaking Channel swims.

With new diets, new superfoods
offering extra vigour and vim,
and spinach claiming that it
really does what it says
on the tin, who knows
what the future holds?

Brian Moses

The Chosen One

I love being chosen
To get the PE kit out

The mats have to be carried (not dragged)
(Miss Moss is very particular about this)
From the store
And the crates with the beanbags and balls
And coloured ribbons
Arranged along the front of the stage
The wall bars swung out and the ropes
   released
And the benches laid in order

And I love being chosen
To put everything away
At the end of the lesson
Everything neatly stacked
In its place
(And sometimes we miss
The first ten minutes of science)

But I'm not so keen
On the bit in between

Roger Stevens

It Always Rains on Sports Day

It always rains on sports day,
or it has for weeks previously,
and we're sitting there on coats
while the grass is steaming.
They might do better to issue us
with floats, to cope with the dozens of puddles
that punctuate our running track.
And the winner might just as well swim home,
where his winner's rosette will be pinned
to a soggy vest.

It's always fun on sports day,
seeing who gets wettest.
You can bet your life
it won't be the teachers –
they come prepared and swan around
beneath their golf umbrellas,
while everyone else is perched on chairs
sinking deeper into the mud.

I hate sports day at our school.
You're out there trying to look cool
in front of parents, brothers, sisters,
grans, grandads, aunts, uncles, cousins,
the lady from two doors down
and your girlfriend from 3C.

And then you slam down in the mud
and you look like a player
in some rugby squad
rather than the bronzed, heroic Greek athlete
that you wanted them to see.

It always rains on sports day,
or it has for weeks previously.

This year it rained so much
that sports day was cancelled.
What a shame!

Brian Moses

Egg and Spoon Race

I've got the right trainers
Got the cool logo
Got the right tracksuit
Got the hip brand
Using free-range eggs – boiled exactly nine
    minutes
Got a top-quality silver-plated spoon
Looking good
So tell me why
I came last in the race?

Roger Stevens

My Javelin

My javelin
Was really travelling
The crowd gave a huge hooray
But it went straight up
And came straight down
Landing only a metre away

My javelin
Was really travelling
There was another big cheer
From the crowd
But unfortunately
It hit a tree
And my throw was disallowed

My javelin
Was really travelling
It shot through the air
Like an arrow
It hit a jet plane
On its way to Spain
And it brought down a duck
And a sparrow

Roger Stevens

Where's the Shot Put?

We were helping sort out the sports store.
Said our teacher Miss Blott, Do you know
Where the shot put got put?
I said, No, but I'll look
Cos I had it a moment ago.

Where did I put the shot put? I asked Scott
Scott said, The shot put? I don't know.
Then I said, It's here!
Miss Blott said, Yeeeeoooowwwweeeeahh!!!!
You've dropped the shot put on my toe.

Roger Stevens

79

Relay Race

Waiting for the baton in the relay race
I'm the third person to run
I'm waiting, I'm waiting, anticipating
I'm going to run faster than a bullet from a
  gun

Here comes number two with the baton
She's running round the track so fast
Look at that speed and she's in the lead
Any moment and then it's my chance

I'm waiting, I'm waiting for the baton
My hand is outstretched and I know
I must take it correctly, my hand's getting
  sweaty
When I grab it I hope she lets go

It's here, it's here. I've got it
Didn't fumble, I grabbed it just right
Now I'm running, I'm running, the crowd are
  all cheering
I'm running with all of my might

My feet are thumping and pounding
I've never before run so fast
But I'm being overtaken, run faster, run
    faster
I was first and I mustn't come last

Number four is ahead and her hand's out
She's reaching, she's reaching . . . Oh my!
The handover's great. She's got it.
She's our fastest. Just look at her fly.

Now I'm sweating, my heart is still thumping
I didn't drop it. And I did my best.
The crowd cheers! We came second.
That's not bad, I reckon.
Now I sit on the grass for a rest.

Roger Stevens

A Sporting Chance

He was the boy who was always left out,
the boy who never made the team,
the boy about whom other boys said,
'We don't want him, you can have him.'

He was the boy who smiled at their jibes,
the boy who laughed along with them,
the boy who pointed a finger at himself,
funny guy, eh?

He was the boy who drew strange faces on his
    books,
faces that resembled the faces of the boys who
    constantly put him down,
the boy who constantly worried his parents:
Seems withdrawn, his reports read. Should
    join in more.

He was the boy who never asked,
'How was the match, how did they do?'
He'd given up trying to be interested by then
and wasn't clued up enough to be taken
    seriously.

Nobody gave him a break on the sports field,
said he was weak, a big mistake,
two left feet, he couldn't play,
put him in goal, no, send him away.

But here's to the team, those talented guys,
here's to the cups and the medals they won.
What fine young sportsmen everyone,
here's to the fun they had.

But the boy who was always left out,
the boy who never made the team
had long ago given up hope
of achieving his sporting dream.

Brian Moses

Disappointment

I am the hand the winner shakes
I am a rain cloud obscuring the sun
I am the lonely runner at the back
I am the stumble at the starter's gun
I am a lost ticket
I am the missed train
I am words of commiseration
I am a muscle strain
I am point-one of one second too long
I am an umpire's bad call
I am a loose arrow, a dropped baton, a
   mistimed swing
I am a miss-hit ball

I am every excuse, and no excuse
For why you lost the game
There is no cup for the runner-up
Disappointment is my name

Roger
Stevens

Salute

The chasm is so much wider,
the fall is so much tougher,
the challenge so much greater,
the road ahead much rougher.

The training much more exhausting,
the setbacks much harder to take,
the path ahead unyielding,
the leap more difficult to make.

So much stamina needed,
so much bravery overcoming pain,
so much strength, so much endurance,
so fantastic to make each gain.

The widest skies in the world
would still not limit their dream.
Everyone, please salute
our Paralympic team.

Brian Moses

Guess the Country

Here's the Olympic motto – Faster, higher,
stronger – translated into fifteen different
languages. It comes from the Latin
Citius, altius, fortius.
Can you guess which each language is?
(Answers on the opposite page)

Vinniger, hoër, sterker
Po-bŭrzo, po-visoka, po-silni
Gèng kuài, gèng gāo, gèng qiáng
Brže, više, jače
Rychleji, výše, silnější
Hurtigere, højere, stærkere
Sneller, hoger, sterker
Nopeammin, korkeammalle, voimakkaammin
Plus rapide, plus haut, plus fort
Schneller, höher, stärker
Tachýtera, psilótera, dynatótera
Tēza, ucca, majabūta
Più veloce, più alto, più forte
Yori hayaku, takaku tsuyoku
Bystryee, vyshe, sil´nyee
Más rápido, más alto, más fuerte
Snabbare, högre, starkare

Roger Stevens

Afrikaans (South Africa)
Bulgarian
Chinese
Croatian
Czech
Danish
Dutch
Finnish
French
German
Greek
Indian
Italian
Japanese
Russian
Spanish
Swedish

And so the poem
Rounds the last bend
Finds the home straight
Past verses fallen by the roadside
Their syntax unravelled
Letters untangled
The poem takes a deep breath
A last swig of water
It's the final stretch
It gains momentum
A last flurry of apposite adjectives
Bold, tired, exhilarated, determined
To the conclusion
The denouement
As gathered stories, plays
And dramas all cheer
The poem crosses the line
Wraps itself in a silver glow
And receives the congratulations
Of friends and family.

Roger Stevens and Brian Moses